Four Super Seasons

WHAT HAPPENS IN
WINTER?

By Alex Appleby

Gareth Stevens
Publishing

Please visit our website, www.garethstevens.com. For a free color catalog of all our high-quality books, call toll free 1-800-542-2595 or fax 1-877-542-2596.

Library of Congress Cataloging-in-Publication Data

Appleby, Alex.
What happens in winter? / by Alex Appleby.
 p. cm. — (Four super seasons)
Includes index.
ISBN 978-1-4824-0114-1 (pbk.)
ISBN 978-1-4824-0116-5 (6-pack)
ISBN 978-1-4824-0113-4 (library binding)
1. Winter — Juvenile literature. I. Appleby, Alex. II. Title.
QB637.8 A66 2014
508.2—dc23

First Edition

Published in 2014 by
Gareth Stevens Publishing
111 East 14th Street, Suite 349
New York, NY 10003

Copyright © 2014 Gareth Stevens Publishing

Editor: Ryan Nagelhout
Designer: Andrea Davison-Bartolotta

Photo credits: Cover, p. 1 Mayovskyy Andrew/Shutterstock.com; p. 5 Nate Allred/Shutterstock.com; pp. 7, 9, 23 iStockphoto/Thinkstock; p. 11 Zurijeta/Shutterstock.com; pp. 13, 24 (snow) FogStock/Thinkstock; pp. 15, 24 (snowmen) Ingram Publishing/Thinkstock; p. 17 Purestock/Thinkstock; p. 19 Jody Dingle/Shutterstock.com; pp. 21, 24 (bear) Lindsay Dean/Shutterstock.com.

Printed in the United States of America

CPSIA compliance information: Batch #CW14GS: For further information contact Gareth Stevens, New York, New York at 1-800-542-2595.

Contents

Winter is a
super season!

It comes after fall.

Winter comes
once a year.

It gets very cold.

It snows in winter.

13

People like
to make snowmen.

They like to ski!

People play ice hockey in winter.

Bears hibernate
to save energy.

21

Spring comes
after winter.

23

Words to Know

bear   snow   snowman

Index